CW00524487

Poet Hazel May Anderson

The Romantic

URBAN RHYMES

AUSTIN MACAULEY PUBLISHERS™
LONDON • CAMBRIDGE • NEW YORK • SHARJAH

A CIP catalogue record for this title is available from the British Library.

ISBN 9781788486293 (Paperback)
ISBN 9781788486309 (Hardback)
ISBN 9781788486316 (ePub e-book)

www.austinmacauley.com

First Published (2019)
Austin Macauley Publishers Ltd
25 Canada Square
Canary Wharf
London
E14 5LQ

To all those fighting climate change, and for a peaceful cleaner planet.

Poems

Introduction

Urban Rhymes *incorporate both a modern street-style poetry and that old style poetry we all know and love.*

Bouncing from climate change, romance, nightclubs, technology and more.

I have undertaken extensive research in regards to some of these pieces, so it is possible to search on ECOSIA search engine, some of the material in this book, due to the key words, search terms and sentences I have used from the people and websites licensed to give me the best information on the subject possible.

Siren

Like a moth drawn to a flame, man just can't resist
Baited, caught, on a line, man is now the fish
Drawn in like a ship to rocks, siren is a calling
Mesmerised is the man, oblivious to all warnings.

Man tries to put a foot down, but what's a boy to do
Woman's running rings, and man ain't got a scooby doo
How can he resist when it's felt in every cell
Woman's given him the fever, all defenses felled.

Data Information Man-chine

Data information, filling brains' expanse
Uploading all the time, we're in a data trance
Data all day long, online till late at night
Not much time to download, at times strung uptight.

Like to see a wander drug
Sold with a Tesla chip

Delving into brain unknown, data the greatest hit
Brain now open wide awake and primed for untold
  download

Accessing unused areas, next step on evolves road
This could cure human condition, on par us with Ai

Same access to the info, man equate immortal life
On par with Ai, now opened up the brain
Projecting to the future, download speeds insane.

The brain is still unrivalled, when measured to machine,
  add some bio interface, hybrid man machine.

Lady of the Pen

Lady of the pen, you got me from the start
Pullin' at my heart strings, tuggin' at my heart
And I love the way you flow and how your ballpoint rolls
Those heart sent lines and words, comin' from your soul.

Manipulate the English language, to images of the mind
Vividly clear and wonderfully sublime.

Thing is I'm the kinda guy whose speech just goes to pot
A short in motor planning, tongue just starts to knot.

But when I start to write, I can conjure a verse
Just know I'm in awe for ever, wherever you're concerned.

Keep writing.

Spring to Spring

Spring time's on its way, still bit chilly though,
But that won't stop the buds, and me thinking what
   to grow ☺
First there is the battle, to claw some garden back,
Overgrown with weeds, days dig I'm back on track

The weather starts to warm, but still a chill at times
Summers closing in, come on summer time
Grass starts to grow like there's no tomorrow ☺,
Can't wait to cut the lawn and trim its winter sorrow

Weather's heating up, it's time for water fights
Day trips to the beach, beach party's at night
Dig out shorts and t-shirts, #need a tan
Glow in the dark white legs, milk white's the shade I am

Beach bum for the summer, explore the English coast
Walk the Cornish coastline and seek out secret coves
Caves and smuggler routes, with tunnels out of sight
Careful where you walk, fall in one you might

6 weeks with the kids, don't wanna give them back
First day of school is here, off they go all packed

Arrival autumns breeze, the leaves are changing colour
Fluttering to the ground, with trees still boasting valour
Trees now in their birthday suits, silent with no leaves
Nights are drawing in now, shortening the eves
28 days till Christmas, not that long to go
The kids are wigging out as winter days go slow

Finally, it's here, and over in a blink,
now it's happy new year, you hear them shout and sing

Glad that it's all over, for another year
Though this year went much quicker, much quicker than
  last year
Couple more months, and spring is here again
The years are moving quicker, the more years that I gain.

Steppin' to the Club

Can I pick you up some time, in my retro car
Whisk you off your feet somewhere, not too far
Arriving at the club, fashionably late
Big up da good man, as we don't do hate.

Standing in the queue feelin' that beat
You by my side looking so sweeeet
Steppin' to the club, headed to the bar
I'll just have a water, babes, I gotta drive the car.

Now we Jack 'n' Jllin' it on the dance floor
Baselines got me rushing, gimme, gimmee more
Find us at the end, chillin' in our zone
On come the lights, everybody home.

Settle in a taxi for the journey back
Anticipation strong, palpitated cardiac
Time to get a grip 'n' fall back in line
Girl are you for real tonight
You've Cinderella blown my mind.

Trippin' on you, in a dream-like state
Just as the taxi man pulls up to the gate
Total English gent, so I've got the door
Offer you my arm as you step out to the floor.

Walk you to the doorstep just to know you're safe
As it's far too dark, and it's far too late
Interest in the air, as we make our way
Potential merging duo, connect in fabrics sway.

Now you're indoors, settled in your home
Left you with my number, funk I hope you phone
But till then for me, a string of sleepless nights
Be my night nurse, and call my cell tonight.

Cosmic Chick

Cosmic chick, yeah she shine up the place
Got a rockin' body and a heavenly face.

Shoots in like a comet, straight from the start
Complete Armageddon, direct to the heart.

Heavenly sound, just like an Angel song
Solar flare, woman's blazin' like a bong.

Top of the charts, she's a number 1 hit
Celestial being, cosmic chick.

Sunset to Sunrise

The land and the trees look so dark
Above it the bright sky forms an arch

Blue gold and orange with a hint of pink
Behind the horizon it starts to sink

Great ball of fire nestling down
And completely free of any sound

Slipping away till the following day
Around the world it continues to stray

As we stand and it disappears
For someone else it re-appears

Returning as slowly as it went away
Here comes a wonderful brand-new day.

Your wish is my command. *It's a boy meets girl thing, I don't know what it is that makes us guys' legs turn to jelly, be nervous and say the complete opposite of what we want when we meet what we perceive to be the one.*

Maybe a chemical reaction in the body, lack of breath, or a concoction of the both. Watch the end few minutes of the film inside out, as they have it perfect.

Your Wish Is My Command

Sometimes when out driving
And feeling a little down
I look into the mirror
I can't shake this stupid frown.

But then I think of you
And the great things that you say
I realise that it's you
Who clears that frown away.

See you have this certain something
A *je ne sais quoi*
That special kind of something
Not found in clubs and bars.

When I see you there
The walls my closest friend
If it didn't have my back
My legs you know they'd bend.

Collapsing to the floor
In a tongue-tied nervous wreck
For you I'd crawl a thousand miles
Just say which way to trek
So now you have the premise
of who and why I am
Just give that lamp a rub girl,
your wish is my command.

Picnic

Shall we go out, it's a lovely day.
Slip on your shoes, I'll whisk you away
Best grab a jumper, we'll go for a stroll
Out in the country, where the hills they do roll
A sandwich, an apple, and a packet of crisps,
bring us a blanket, we'll have a picnic
You pick the spot, I'll trample the ground,
listen to that, can't hear a sound.

Drop Top

Summer's here, so we're droppin' down the hoods
Don't leave the house, till you know you're looking good
Pair of nice shoes, freshly ironed top
Gonna be seen, on it like white hot.

Roof down drop top, drivin' through the town
Taking it easy, seeing who's around
Sun's getting brighter, on go the shades
Drivin' to the country, through the summer haze.

On the way home, stop in to the local
Gotta be good, #onepint total
Chatting at the bar, been a long week
Little bit of banta, bit of tongue and cheek.

Finish off the pint, must be on our way
Be a good lad, and play another day
Nice to be home, in your own domain
Blazin' in the sun, or chill with Mary Jane.

In come the clouds, then it starts to pour
Smell that summer rain, as many times before
Indoors for some telly, or some GTA
Bottle of wine or beer, to finish off the day
Quench that evening thirst, with your favourite bev
Reflecting on the day, as you rest your head.

Moving Things
Don't Gather Moss

There is a bouncing bumblebee
Buzzing around you and me
Now you see him, now you don't
He'll disappear, no he won't
Things seem brighter, when he's there
No one can think about their cares
He doesn't stay, enough to bore,
when he leaves, we're left wanting more
He'll never be rich, because
moving things don't gather moss
But we love him, rich or poor,
one good thing he's not a bore.

Hazel May Anderson, Nan

When I have a problem or a repetitive thought bothering me, I place it at the forefront of my mind, take a big breath and sigh it out, then breathe in fresh air and replace the thought with a positive thought. Takes some practice, although a drink or smoke usually helps. No use worrying about something that hasn't happened yet, or crying over spilt milk.

When Things
Don't Seem to Be

When things don't seem to be, working out for me,
I get my life and flip side, to see what comes to me.

I can't always be right, or get my own way,
so I take a deep breath, and here is what I pray.

Thanks for all the things that have landed next to me
even know I'm down, deep breath I can now see.

All the love and happiness that has been placed here
 with me,
I can't believe my luck in life,
I feel so light and free.

Good

Sometimes, when a good thing comes along,
you're walking on air, and you can't do no wrong.

Sometimes, a good thing can go bad for you,
Don't give up, on the good things, even when you're blue.

And let's just say, you wanna leave the hood
Be proactive and apply some good.

Stay strong guys and see it through, the light is just over the
    other side, failing that G>O>O>D
Get, Out, Of, Dodge:
To leave unnoticed, unexpectedly and fast from an
    undesired location and surroundings.
There's a whole world out there, new people, new
    surroundings can be so refreshing.

Fwork

Is this my life, fworking till the end
Get to touch the money, but all we do is spend
Around and round again, I'd give it up today
WTF's the point? And all those bills to pay.

And we could all live for free
Check out The Venus project.

A Beautiful Day

I sit in the conservatory and watch my girls play
One on the swing, it's a beautiful day
Julie pushing round teddy on the red car
Around the garden but must seem so far.

Come on, Dad high up to the sky,
push me some more I want to fly.
Lilly's a bird high in the trees,
swinging so high who knows what she sees.

Now in their house playing with dolls
In the backfield is a beautiful foal
Snorting as it rolls 'round on its back
Neighing occasionally what a good scratch.

The clouds draw in, in comes the shade
C'mon girls let's all pack away.

Dad, Dad just one more go
So I push her on the swing to and throw
Julie wants a push in the car
Once round the garden must seem so far.

Got them indoors with some colouring books
Smells like rain, and that's how the sky looks
Still, we're in England, what do I expect,
time for hot chocolate then off to bed.

Money's a Stranger: *I wrote this during a period when I was losing my job with an infrastructure company.*

I have incorporated the effect that being jobless can have on a family. Especially the children who really need to know it's not their fault, as they sometimes think it is. Best not to argue out in the open, 'save it for in the car'.

Money's a Stranger

Down on my luck, can't seem to climb out
Just as I do, another thing sprouts
Money's a stranger, as far as I see
Got up and run off, seems it's left me.

Grumps with my kids, they don't understand
Must look back, to when I held my dad's hand
I would look to him with admiralty
The best in the world that's what I must be.

Un-wavered and a tower of strength though I'm
Sinking and can swim no more lengths
Don't be so hard when they don't obey
Just take a deep breath and here's what I'll say.

I need you to listen and I'll tell you how,
a smile and a hug will help us now
I just needed to let you know why
it's important for us to see eye to eye.

Now I must chase up, that money that's left
Because in your future I need to invest.

The Great Wood

This story is from so very, so very long ago
about the great wood, I think we all should know.

Jon o' Groats to Land's End, it's said a squirrel walked
through trees that grew together, branch overlapped and
  taught.

Of our ancient isle, from one end to the other,
abundant habitats, when nature was our mother.

Industrial Revolution, post the great Crusades,
up until these points in time great wood stayed unscathed.

Unused now is the land, whence the great wood stood,
terra form the unused fields, replant the great wood.

Inspired by climate change and global warming,

I am a proud owner of 2 acres of forest, my section provides thousands of pounds of O_2 per year and digests tons of carbon. I firmly believe due to building, farming, ship-building and industrial revolution etc. that a majority of the trees on planet Earth have been felled and not replaced. There wasn't the scientific data to refer to back then, and people just didn't know deforestation to be a problem.

But now we do have the data and could reverse the effects of climate change simply by covering the planet in green. Darwin and the British Navy terraformed Ascension Island with the help of wisely gardens, so there is no reason why our generations can't do it today.

Low growing ferns and palms that require little water were used.

Genetic engineering could help too, and machines designed to strip plant could play a big part along with people paid to plant and water trees in the initial stages of growth.

The new trees will provide O_2, digest carbon and store it in the wood, it will stop land erosion and provide food.

But most importantly, it will create shade, absorbing the sun's heat and harmful rays instead of deflecting it upwards and in turn, cool the rivers that feed the oceans.

I saw a thing on a documentary, that when cells in a petri dish are starved of 60% oxygen or less, cells become cancerous.

We are still made of cells, right?

So due to the deforestation and other human activity, carbon emissions etc., does the present day breathable atmosphere have less than bare minimum 60%, that we need to support healthy cells.

Only 12.9 % of Britain is forest and woodland now.

Do the math; if it takes 1 acre of trees for approx. 18 people's oxygen per year, and there are 7.7 billion people on the planet, and:

Total land surface area approximately: 57,308,738 square miles.
Approx. 33% is desert.
Approx. 24% is mountainous.
Subtracting this uninhabitable 57% (32,665,981 mi2)
So from the total land area that leaves us with 24,642,757 square miles or 15.77 billion acres of habitable land.

That would leave us with approx. 2 acres to every person less the land we have built on, and the land that is now poisoned.

We also need to subtract all farmland that is needed to supply food to the human race,

I would say it is cutting it very fine if not already at tipping point.

And in addition to all that there is the rising sea levels to take into consideration, how much of the above will end up below sea level.

Ascension Island
Planet Earth
Strip Planting Not
Strip Mining

It takes 2 trees a year just for 2 people's O_2
One acre of trees a year, air for eighteen of you.

Absorbing tons of carbon, they store within their wood
Gives thousand pounds of O_2, all they do is good.

A tree's height promotes rain, when felled brings climate
   change
In the shade is 6 degrees cooler, stop felling trees for trade.

Strip planting not strip mining, this could pave the way
Darwin terraformed island, in months then sailed away
With today's technology, can plant them anywhere
Oasis garden of Eden, ten years' earth repaired.

Climate change reversal, defo up to us
Fixed within our life time, Earth repaired by us
Rivers need the shade, to cool the warming oceans
Rivers running cooler, ocean cooling potion.

Without the trees to shade, the heat reflects on up
Trapped by the carbon, the climate it corrupts
Easily it's fixed, Ascension Island Earth
Cover her with green, let the trees gain girth
More aged be the tree, the more good that it will do
Don't put back the trees, we could all be through.

Q: What will Ai specify, that us humans do?
A: Put back all the trees, that the planet grew.

We should not stop there, we need so many more
Strip planet Earth, till green, all corners four.

Stumblin' to the Club

Finally I've finished work, it's been a long week,
Pop into the pub now, grab a pint sweeet.

Dress to look a1, in case the club we hit,
Gotta look smooth, so you own that sh*t.

When you've finished work, pop down to the pub,
A pint O'beer or two, grab some pub grub.

Or get a change of clothes, go and have a wash,
Forget the pub grub, pop out grab some posh.

Tryin' to keep in line, got money I need to save,
But marching gears online, and the lads are feeling brave
Had a couple now, here come the babes,
dragged off to the club, some things never change.

Stumble to the club, the door men look unsure,
Still they let us in, as I back-handed him a score.

Steppin' to the club, work it as I walk,
Moving to the sounds, let that body talk.

Movin' to the bar, I'll just have a bex,
Holdin' up the bar, whilst I'm givin' it some flex.
Suddenly the shots, whose idea was this
Any more of that, I'm walking home pissed.

The girls are out in force tonight, looking so damn fine
Aroma as they pass me by, I wish they all were mine.

Confidence is peaking, 'ere we bloody go
Off to the floor, come enjoy the show.

Rollin' solo on the dance floor, shufflin' for a space
This line never fails, babes im sure I know your face.

She tries to shout her name out, but can't hear a funking'
    thing
Names can be for later, it's a night club ting.

Love Lost

I want to stop loving you, but I'm in too deep,
Up to my neck in it, tied at the feet.

Eating me like cannibals, God I'm in a stew,
Up the creek, lost the paddle, without a way to you.

Blindsided me, you caught me off my guard,
Trapped in your high beam, hit by your car.

I'm nothing when you're not here, it's like I don't exist,
Wandering aimlessly, lost in Abyss.

Bottom of the trench, with 7 miles to surface,
Don't know which way is up no more, no longer
  serving purpose.

The Church Bells of This Village

The bells of this village are raining on me
Heaven sent I think and in perfect harmony

Sailing on the wind, floating on the breeze
Not too long or loud, just enough to please

Mixing with the sound, of wind kissed blowing Willows
All across the village, this ancient sound does Mellow.

One Pointedness Mind Controlsss

Go out and be awesome when you're feeling down
Running or a bike ride will help you lift that frown.

Don't be half glass empty, be a half glass full
It's the angle of perception, that makes it all be cool.

Repetitive thoughts? Then learn to meditate
Practise some one pointedness, make mind elevate.

Flip the situation, just like heads and tails
Keep to the good path, and good
Sure, they may return, be strong and just ignore,
   always prevails.

Struggling at the start, battling crappy thoughts, sort them
   singularly, like on trial inside a court.

You're the judge and the jury, bad thoughts eradicate
Imagine your mind's a garden, kick bad thoughts out
   the gate.

Replace bad ones with some good ones, like old food at the
   store.
In your mind just picture 1, for long breath you intake
The same when you exhale, just 1, that's meditate.

Concentrate on one, whilst breathing in and out no room
   left for bad thoughts, distinguish them with clout.

Practise some one pointedness, whenever there is chance,
Battling those unwanted thoughts, take a steadfast stance.

Hatred kills the hater, all hate get rid of it
Forgive and try to forget, we're all capable of it.

It don't do you no good, carrying bad thoughts around
A few weeks of one pointedness, mind starts to
    become sound.

Add a little exercise, clears mind and body too,
Go out and be awesome, proceed your whole life through.

Try to use traffic jams, or when you hit red lights, the
    perfect opportunity, practise day and night
Bring thought to forefront of mind, release the biggest sigh
As well as some one pointedness, relax, enjoy the ride.

For the entire inward breath think one
For the entire outward breath think one
This is based on researching the science of breath.
A minute in the morning and a minute in the evening are
    all that are needed.

One Pointedness Explained

To practise one pointedness, inhale a long slow breath through the nose and regulate it like a tap with the throat, to steady its flow.

For the whole intake of the breath stare at or picture a number one or a dot, and for the whole outlet of the breath think a long-winded 1, thus thinking 1 for the whole time, there for not allowing any other thoughts to enter the mind for the duration. And repeat again and again.

Before you start, breathe out all your air and as you inhale, gently push the stomach out to draw the air using the diaphragm first to inflate the base of the lung then inflate chest.

When exhaling, gently pull diaphragm in first to draw the air from bottom of lungs then finally the chest.

This allows the mind to clear and retain one thought only. 1.

Also allowing the mind to declutter and to be defragmented, with continued practice your mind becomes strong and able to eradicate problems and repetitive thoughts almost instantly.

It is also the first time in your life that your eyes remain still.

It certainly doesn't do anyone any good carrying all that mind clutter about.

This Message I Do Send

Keep it up Dad, you've always got my back
Life isn't always easy
Can be a right old bumpy track

I am you in spirit, just driving up the lane
I will get there in there in the end, even in this rain

I know I'm taking time, just a few more twists and bends
So, with this hand I write, this message I do send

We all love you dearly, you should know this now
And thanks for all the guidance and trying to show us how.

Hybrid

Supernova hybrid, magma to the core,
Sundance Kid, quick on the draw.

Electrified effect, arcing from the source
when you hear the lyrics, experience the force.

Fleet as the wind, glides in like a swift,
speeding up the highway, cornering with drift.

Negotiating English, an English gent don't slate,
givin' it some boom ting, Red Bull aviate.

Love at First Sight

Love at first sight girl, what's a boy to do,
Fool's in deep, now he's met you.
Down in the first round of his biggest fight,
the man has just been KO'd by love at first sight.

Many fall in love or build it as they go,
 that's just not the case for me, I'm not the average Joe.
I'll try and give an insight of how it is for me,
as soon as I see the one, it's love immediately.

In how many does it exist, there's just no way to know,
immediate love thing, shot from cupid's bow.
Inconsistent heartbeats, right up to the throat,
beating to new rhythms, heart's new love beat notes.

New love beating heart, speech just goes to pot,
from the very start, till it wants to stop.
Something else takes over, an underlying force,
now in auto pilot, it sets out its own course.

Absolutely no control, completely out of my hands,
a short in motor planning, no longer in command.
Second to none, rivalled by no other,
trust me with your heart, girl, cos I got it covered.

Cat

Wanna have some fun,
you just gotta say.
Your cat's lying here,
waiting for his play.

You left me long time ago,
so I sleep and dream.
In the land of never never,
with you, my feline queen.

If I'm asleep, then wake me up,
we'll play the night away.
This cat sleeps whenever,
but any time's for play.

You're Purrrr-fect!

London Ting *is written about a trip to London I took years ago to get some decent vinyl from Camden Town.*

Tried to incorporate the walking, bus and tube you need to use to get around town.

London Ting

Goin' up town, London thing
Steppin' to da beatz, English ting
Right vibes playin', got it going on
New creps jeans, head phones on

Bare-looking tan, looking kinda brown
Headin' up the road, into London town
London can be friendly, even cold as ice
Nice to be important, more important to be nice

Across the Tower Bridge, onto Leister Square
Hop onto the tube, return fair
Street artists and painters, the arts are all around
Catch a double decker, into Camden town.

Record store with vinyl's, bustin' out the sounds
Flicking through their records, till the right one's found
3 for price of 2, got a wicked deal
Play them when I'm home, old school wheels of steel.

Fake Tan

My old mate, whilst out he met a chic,
They got on so well, it turned out to be a hit.

Went back to his house and turned off all the lights,
a huggin' and a kissin', a nibble and a bite.

When suddenly he tasted a right old funny taste,
he went off to the toilet, steppin' with post haste.

Lookin' to the mirror, fake tan up the place,
got the toothbrush out, cleaning his boatrace.

When he went back in and turned on all the lights,
my poor old mate got a great big fright.

The funny thing was, the lady that he met
had only fake tanned parts, arms, legs, face and neck.

He took another look, the rest of her was pale,
when telling me the story, I asked, "Bruv, did you bail?"

"Don't be silly, boy, I have got a heart,
I ate some more fake tan, finish what you start."

Long Live Hooky Street *was written with our favourite geeza in mind, Del Boy, I have tried to modernise Hooky Street.*

Long Live Hooky St

Direct from the hood, roll cold as ice,
Little bit of naughty, and a little bit of nice.
Rising from the streets, you get to know the lingo,
Just made a call, long time ting though.

Make another call, man about a dog,
Checking what he's got, and what he wants to flog,
There's mp3s and DVDs, fake designer clothes,
No money back no guarantee, that's just the way it goes.

Tell you what I'll take the lot, if you sweeten up the deal,
I'll chuck these in, best I can do, you got 'em for a steal
So, I drop the lot to bob the shop, he'll lose that in a week,
All is good within the hood, long live Hooky Street.

Down in Waltham Row

There are lots and lots of schools, all across the earth
Some of them are made of concrete bricks and turf

But there's these ones we go, in Waltham Sherlock Row
that has inside these teachers I think you all should know

They have this certain way of teaching all our kids
To the highest of degrees, in this I tell no fibs

Painting art and colouring, adding playing stories
Come and see these ladies work, and our kids in all
  their glories

Running all around, jumping up and down
Keeping up their spirits, we never see a frown

So, a big well done ladies, for passing on your ways
You're the best in all the land, there's not much more to say.

Rollin' Solo

Don't want the phone to ring or anyone to call,
chillin' on my own tonight, that's how I like to roll.

I learned a long time ago, enjoy one's company,
no need to entertain, just kick back, get comfy.

No need to be concerned, on how I look tonight,
just chillin' with the still, down low with the lights.

Listen to some chill, or some dinner jazz,
Hungry House, Just Eat, curry's what I'll have.

Bling goes the door bell, play that DVD,
got a new release today, one I haven't seen.

Eyes Wide Shut's the feeling, light weight, solo host,
noddy at home noddin', as I start to doze.

Sparked till 3 am, film went 'round twice more,
didn't hear a thing, bet they did next door.

Best finish off the film, as now I'm wide awake,
goin' in for seconds, cold curry on a plate.

Out for just the sake of it is not all it's about,
stay in and roll solo, you and just your house.

Who needs friends around tonight, your bestie's sitting
    here,
book a night in with yourself, your night to engineer.

Lady A Woman of Refinement

Honed to perfection, like a fine wine
Sweet to the palate, somewhat dry at times
Centre of attention, when entering the room
But when she goes to leave, it always feels too soon.

Angel on the wing, glides across the floor
A pleasure to be near, leaves you craving more
Holds her own in public, conducts with honesty
Strait-laced, all in order, elegance's treat.

Positive and focused, ballet poise like flow
Radiating warmth, with her sunshine glow
No facade in sight, lady shinin' true
Casual, smart or gown, lady through and through.

Lives throughout life, to do the right thing
Compassionate intentions, she'll end your suffering
A woman of refinement, persona finely tuned, scanning the
   horizon, for gentleman attuned.

When finally he arrives, appealing true her heart
True love's serenade, Amadeus Mozart.
Two become one, their destinies entwine
Let Loves blossom fragrance, plume till the end of time.

Love can conquer death, at least that's what they say.
Soul mates are for ever, let love guide the way.

Hooky St
Continued

People may frown, but WTF can we do
I've applied for a hundred jobs, maybe even two

The people at the bottom, getting poorer every year
"We have to make more budget cuts," that's all we ever hear

Funny though, and how bizarre, it don't affect the rich,
Seems to be those at the bottom, who's always
  getting stitched

Can't blame the youth, who grew up skint, for taking what
  they want,
Rubbed in their face, for years on telly, a never-
  ending taunt

It's human nature to want, what other people's got,
Even if it ain't top notch, and feels a little hot

As long as we get to look and dress like stars
The sting of being poor subsides and we feel on par
Given everyone had an equal start and chance

I believe those at the bottom would seriously advance
Need money to make some money, so the story goes

But at the mo I've got a score, can't even buy some shoes
So make a call to my guy, to see what's in today
He's got a bit of this bit of that, not back till end of play
Money's still printed right? Bit coin, or string of code

If we were all free from debt, positive we would bode
When I see a shooting star, I know for what ill wish
A hundred grand for each of us, the government
  should dish.

Interplanetary Species

Man equate the speed of light, populating planets far
Soon it'll take us just a day, in speed of light cars.

Pull up near a local sun, photon charged light drive
Spread planetary species, all planets far and wide.

Out breed the longest flights, like rabbit to the fox
Extend out to the furthest systems, switch to light speed
  clock.

Wander drugs and upgrades, to help on man's great quest,
geneticists and engineers, tweak man till at his best.

Intergalactic species, spread with multitude,
Terraforming geo spheres, abundances of food.

Interplanetary species, evolve from human race,
Outwitting the impossible, and Google miles of space.

Flight Wright
Written by Alaine12

Higher than a kite
Or even a bird
Flying so high
Quite cool, words.

With dreams to reach the heavens
Loving all the views
Things to see, like bright blue seas
And all because of you.

Trixi Hazel

I love my cat, she's good to me,
Sits on my lap, feels so silky.

When I let her out, off she goes,
Into the shed, to have a nose.

I shake the biscuits, she comes running in,
I put the biscuits down and open up the tin.

Then we let her out, to go to the loo,
Because she probably needs a poo.

So-Cal Hottie

The flight from LA to UK, So Cal hottie's next to me
At first she chattin' on her phone, could be love or just
  family.

I was about to turn and say something, but I dunno bro
Something arose inside of me, if I could leave I'd up and go.

I figured watch some free films, no way she's into me
I'll just kick back and freeze in time, spin some DVDs
You know a little later when the steward brought our food.

She turned with dessert and said to me, "Would you like
  mine too?"
I accepted hottie's gift, but I just had to ask her why.
She replied, "I don't eat sweets," now hottie don't seem shy
We only said a few more words all throughout the flight.
And when we landed in UK *whoosh* hottie's out of sight.

The moral of this story, has gotta go like this: to all my bros
  and hotties jot them digits on a slip.
Don't miss that opportunity to hand your cell and link
Write it, fold it, hand it, and don't you over think...

Born in 1974, grew up in an old Edwardian house, 30 miles southeast of London. Raised in army town Aldershot due to my nan, granddad and my dad all being in the army.

As I grew up, I listened to chart music on a record player with radio and would try and copy the older lads down the park, body-popping and breakdancing, with a piece of lino, and a portable tape deck stereo.

Punks and mods were still about, and for me, Adam Ant was the man back then.

I used to spend time with my nan, she was a great teacher and mentor, utilising her calm persona to connect and open my mind to writing poetry, and the art of enjoying and utilising one's own company.

A poem can be like an ice carving, keep chipping away at it until it is perfect.

At other times, it can be almost instantaneous, and fall into your lap, almost as if the words are arcing from an unknown source.

Be the writer at all times, don't just look, observe, as inspiration can spring from the most unlikely people, places and day-to-day happenings.

Remember: Manners maketh man.
Credit to William Hormon.

Nice to be important, but more important to be nice.
Credit to Roger Federer and Walter Winchel.